Don't F@&K Up Your Job Interviews

By

Nicholas T. Rustad, MBA

V3

DISCLAIMER: The information provided in this book is based on the experience of Nicholas and his team at CoreTactic LLC and is not intended to be a substitute for professional advice from a legal, financial, or medical expert. CoreTactic and Nicholas Rustad are not liable for any use of this information.

Dear Readers,

Congratulations! You have just picked up a powerful tool that will transform your job interview experiences. Whether you are a fresh graduate stepping into the professional world or a seasoned executive seeking new horizons, this book is your compass to navigate the intricate landscape of interviews.

"Don't F@&K Up Your Job Interviews" is not just another guide; it is your secret weapon. Here is what awaits you within these pages:

The Art of Preparation:

Discover how meticulous research can set you apart. We delve into understanding company culture, mission statements, and recent achievements. Remember, knowledge is your armor.

Crafting Your Strategy:

Interviews are battles of strategy. Learn how to create an elevator pitch that leaves an impression. Nail those behavioral questions using the STAR method. And yes, we will decode the mysterious salary negotiation dance.

Practice Makes Perfect – sort of:

Rehearse aloud, visualize success, and embrace the power of positive psychology. We will even explore color psychology (because yes, black matters!).

The Curious Mind Asks:

At the end of every interview lies an excellent opportunity: your chance to ask questions. We will guide you through thoughtful inquiries about team dynamics, company culture, and industry trends.

Bonus Round: Psychological Hacks:

Ever wondered about the best interview time? Or how body language influences perception? We have you covered with psychological tips that will give you the edge.

Remember, interviews are not mere conversations; they are gateways to your dreams. So, grab your highlighter, bookmark your favorite sections, and let us embark on this transformative journey together.

Wishing you confidence, clarity, and countless "You're hired!" moments.

Nicholas Todd Rustad, MBA

Table of Contents

Chapter 1: Overview

First, there is no such thing as a perfect interview. I have received countless questions from my clients, coworkers, and friends about the proper way to give a job interview. There are at least one million different opinions about how to be successful with a job interview. The best person that does the best interview wins the job. Obviously, you are going to want to make sure that they have the skills, but if you nail an interview, you have an exceptionally good chance of getting the job. Please do not overthink this, you will get better with practice.

Before the interview, invest time in understanding the company's mission, values, and recent achievements. Explore their website, social media, and press releases. Familiarize yourself with the interviewers' backgrounds too.

In addition, when asked, "Tell me about yourself," you will want to deliver a succinct elevator pitch that conveys why you are perfect for this job based on your past experience. You will want to highlight your relevant skills, experiences, and how you align with the company's goals, BUT in a way that is humble and positive.

Next, print out the job description and underline specific skills the employer seeks. Think of examples from your past work that demonstrate these skills. It is also an exceptionally good idea to run the job description and your resume through a website called job scan and you can access it by going to jobscan.co. At the back of the book is a link to sign up for your own account, and you will receive ten free scans. All other free accounts will only be able to scan five times.

The most popular type of question in a job interview is based on behavior. You will know that you have a behavioral question because they typically start off with "please tell me about a time when you…." The interviewer is looking at your past behavior because that will help to determine how you will perform in the job. The whole premise of behavioral questions is that past behavior dictates future performance. So, some key tips here when you are answering a behavioral question. You are going to want to use the star method, which is situation, task, action, result. The star method will help to make sure that your answers are succinct and easy to understand for your interviewer.

Here is how to prepare for behavioural questions by using the STAR method:

- Situation: Describe the context.

- Task: Explain what needed to be done.

- Action: Detail the steps you took.

- Result: Share the positive outcome.

Rehearse your answers with a friend or even to yourself. Speaking aloud helps solidify your responses and boosts confidence.

Be ready to discuss salary expectations. Use tools like Indeed's Salary Calculator to determine an appropriate range based on your location and experience.

At the end of the interview, ask insightful questions about the role, team dynamics, and company culture. Show genuine interest.

Remember, each interview is an opportunity to showcase your skills and personality. Good luck!

Chapter 2: Research the Company and Interview Data

If you want to elevate your game and stand out amongst the other applicants for the position, you will want to research the company's background, their mission and vision. The more that you can demonstrate that you have done the research, you are interested in the company, and you are interested in the role it is going to help position you to get the job.

Here are several key areas to check out:

Mission and Values:

Begin by comprehending the company's mission statement and core values. These provide insights into their overall purpose and the principles they uphold.

Recent Achievements:

Investigate recent milestones, product launches, or awards the company has received.

This demonstrates that you're up-to-date and genuinely interested.

Company Culture:

Explore their website for information on company culture. Look for clues about work environment, employee testimonials, and any unique initiatives they promote.

Dive into Their Website:

The About Us section is important to understand their history, founders, and key milestones.

Products and Services:

Familiarize yourself with their offerings. Know what they sell, produce, or provide.

News and Press Releases:

Check for recent news articles or press releases. This helps you stay informed about their current activities.

Social Media Presence:

LinkedIn®: Follow the company on LinkedIn. Read their posts, articles, and employee profiles.

Twitter®, Facebook®, Instagram®: Explore their social media channels. Look for updates, engagement with followers, and any relevant industry content they share.

LinkedIn® Profiles:

Find the LinkedIn profiles of your interviewers and see if you can find a common ground. Understand their roles, backgrounds, and any common connections you might have.

Google® Search:

Search their names online. You might discover additional information or shared interests.

LinkedIn Sales Navigator®:

LinkedIn Sales Navigator is a great tool when researching companies and their activities. This tool can show you overall company hiring patterns that can help to explain their current health.

Remember, thorough research not only impresses interviewers but also equips you to ask insightful questions during the interview.

Chapter 3: Your Elevator Pitch

I cannot overly stress how important the elevator pitch is, in your interview. I think of it as setting the stage. You are setting the stage for the conversation to give the interviewer a sense of who you are and what you are most proud of in your career. Personally, for me when I interview potential employees, I really want to hear a cheerful outlook, someone who is confident in their abilities and able to talk about what they achieved freely parent Let us dive deeper into crafting an effective elevator pitch for job interviews. When you're asked, "Tell me about yourself," follow these steps to create a memorable and impactful introduction:

Your Three Things:

To create an inspiring elevator pitch, first, think about three things that you are most proud of in terms of accomplishment, reward, honor. Once you have those three things, we are going to build an elevator pitch that will get people's attention. For example, my three things are I want a marathon, I was the first in my family to achieve an undergraduate and graduate degree, and I have over 25 years of information technology leadership experience.

Start with a Hook:

Begin with a concise and attention-grabbing opening. Imagine you're stepping into an elevator with a potential employer, and you have only 30 seconds to make an impression.

Example: "Hi, I'm [Your Name]. As a seasoned software engineer with a passion for creating user-friendly applications, I've successfully delivered projects for Fortune 500 companies."

Highlight Relevant Skills:

Mention the key skills that directly relate to the job you're interviewing for. Be specific and avoid generic statements.

Example: "My expertise lies in full-stack development using Python, JavaScript, and React. Recently I built a scalable web application with optimized database performance."

Showcase Relevant Experiences:

Briefly touch on your professional journey. Highlight experiences that align with the role you're pursuing.

Example: "In my previous role at XYZ Corp, I led a cross-functional team to launch a mobile app that increased user engagement by 30%. I thrive in collaborative environments."

Connect to Company Goals:

Tailor your pitch to the company you're interviewing with. Show that you've done your homework and understand their mission.

Example: "I'm excited about [Company Name]'s commitment to sustainability. As someone who values eco-friendly practices, I'd love to contribute to your green initiatives."

End with Enthusiasm:

Conclude your pitch with enthusiasm and a call to action. Express your eagerness to learn more about the company and contribute.

Example: "I'm thrilled about the opportunity to join [Company Name]. I'm confident that my skills in [specific area] align perfectly with your team's goals."

Remember, practice your elevator pitch until it flows naturally. Customize it for each interview and adapt based on the role and company.

What are your three things?

What is your draft pitch?

Chapter 4: The Job Description

One of the first things you will want to do is to analyze the Job Description. This is your source of all information related to this company and position, to start! You will learn more. You will want to read it thoroughly and do not skim! Read it very carefully to understand the role's responsibilities, expectations, and qualifications.

Personally, when I am hiring someone, if they ask me a question and the answer is on the job description, it is a no go for me, at that point. This signals that you did not prepare for the interview. I do not want to hire an employee that does not thoroughly do the research and knows what they are getting into. If I sense that they did not read the job description I am going to be concerned that they do not know what they are getting into, they may not be prepared for the role, and I may have to rehire in three to six months.

Finding those "focus words". These are keywords that you can leverage to set yourself apart from other candidates. The more keyword matches you have in your resume, the better.

WARNING: POTENTIAL F'UP

Keep in mind that we have different words for different things, another word for this is semantics. Customer service may be in the job description but in your history, you may have called it customer success. You will want to change the words around in your resume to match what is in the job description, in terms of semantics. The person reviewing your resume will only look at it for about 8 seconds, if there is anything on the resume that causes a question, a pause, or needing to follow up it will thank your application.

Identify keywords related to skills, qualifications, and experience. These are essential for aligning your application with the employer's requirements.

Now Let's Break Down the Job Description:

Tasks and Responsibilities:

Pay attention to the specific tasks listed, and the semantics. What will you be doing day-to-day? Highlight these and ensure they match with your resume, even down to the exact words.

Qualifications and Skills:

Note the desired qualifications (education, certifications) and skills (technical, soft). These are your targets.

Underline Relevant Skills:

As you read, underline skills that resonate with your background. These are your selling points.

Provide Evidence:

Think of examples from your past work that demonstrate these skills. Be ready to share specific achievements or projects.

Prioritize Skills:

If you possess multiple skills, prioritize the ones most relevant to the job. Highlight these prominently in your resume and cover letter.

Customize Your Application:

Tailor your application and resume for each job. Use the same language as the job description to show alignment and run your resume through jobscan.co to ensure it will match up well with the recruiter's job description.

Quantify Your Impact:

Quantifiable results are important, they include measurable results. For instance, "Increased sales by 20%," or "Reduced customer response time by 30%."

Remember, understanding the job description not only helps you tailor your application but also prepares you for interviews. Reflect on which themes, skills, and keywords pertain to you, and weave them into your materials.

Chapter 5: THE STAR METHOD

Let's dive into the S.T.A.R. method for handling behavioural questions during job interviews. S.T.A.R. stands for Situation, Task, Action, and Result, and it is a method for answering questions. It will help to ensure you listener receives the information in the right order, and also keep them engaged. This structured approach helps you provide clear and compelling answers. Here is an example of how to use the S.T.A.R. method.

Q: Tell us about a time when you had a disagreement with a co-worker, what happened?

A: Great question, as I think back in my career, I have not had a lot of conflict or confrontation with co-workers, but there was this one situation I can share. (Situation) I was working for an online college, and one day I missed a meeting with a colleague to discuss some IT support options. (Task) After I emailed and apologized to him, his supervisor was still not happy with me, so she asked me to apology to my colleague in front of the whole team. (Action) I was so irritated at this situation, that I asked the supervisor if we could have a private conversation. (Result) She didn't realize that I was under tremendous amounts of stress, and I simply overslept. She explained her behaviour and we agreed to communicate more and appear unified. (noticed how I ended on a positive outcome, always try to do that with any and all answers in an interview)

Situation (S): Describe the Context

Set the Scene: Begin by explaining the situation or context. What was the challenge or scenario you faced?

Be Specific: Provide enough details to help the interviewer understand the context.

Example (S): "During my internship at XYZ Company, we were tasked with improving customer satisfaction scores."

Task (T): Explain What Needed to Be Done

Define Your Role: Describe your specific role or responsibility within the situation.

Highlight the Objective: Explain what goal or task you needed to accomplish.

Example (T): "My task was to analyse customer feedback data and identify areas for improvement."

Action (A): Detail the Steps You Took

Break Down Your Actions: Describe the specific steps you took to address the situation.

Emphasize Your Contribution: Highlight your individual actions and decision-making process.

Example (A): "I conducted a thorough analysis of survey responses, identified common pain points, and collaborated with the product team to design targeted solutions."

Result (R): Share the Positive Outcome

Quantify the Impact: Explain the positive results of your actions. Use metrics or specific achievements.

Highlight Your Contribution: Show how your efforts directly led to the outcome.

Example (R): "As a result of our changes, customer satisfaction scores increased by 20%, and we received positive feedback from our users."

Remember, practice using the STAR method with different scenarios from your past experiences. It helps you structure your answers and showcase your problem-solving abilities effectively.

Prepared next is a list of common behavioural questions, practice them with a friend or family member. Here's a compilation of common behavioural questions you might

encounter during an interview:

Q: Tell me about a time when you had to work effectively

in a team.

TIP: Share a specific example of collaborating with others,

resolving conflicts, or achieving a common goal.

Q: Describe a situation where you faced a challenge or

obstacle at work. How did you overcome it?

TIP: Highlight your problem-solving skills and resilience

in handling difficult situations.

Q: Give an example of a project or task where you

demonstrated leadership.

TIP: Discuss how you motivated others, made decisions, and led by example.

Q: Tell me about a time when you had to adapt to change or unexpected circumstances.

TIP: Explain how you adjusted your approach, stayed flexible, and maintained productivity.

Q: Share a story about a successful client interaction or customer service experience.

TIP: Emphasize your communication skills, empathy, and ability to meet client needs.

Q: Describe a situation where you had to prioritize tasks or manage your time effectively.

TIP: Illustrate your organizational skills and time management abilities.

Q: Have you ever worked on a cross-functional project? How did you collaborate with different teams?
TIP: Discuss your ability to bridge gaps between departments and achieve common objectives.

Q: Tell me about a time when you received constructive feedback. How did you handle it?
TIP: Show your openness to learning and willingness to improve based on feedback.

Q: Share an experience where you had to meet tight deadlines. How did you handle the pressure?

TIP: Highlight your ability to work efficiently under stress.

Q: Describe a situation where you had to resolve a conflict with a co-worker or team member.

TIP: Discuss how you approached the issue, communicated, and found a resolution.

Remember, the key to answering behavioural questions is to provide specific examples from your past experiences. Use the STAR method (Situation, Task, Action, Result) to structure your responses and showcase your skills effectively.

Chapter 6: Practice Makes Perfect – sort of

I dislike the name of this chapter of the book, nothing in this world is perfect, but I could not think of a better title, since everyone knows this phase so we will run with it for now. My point is that I want you to think about what is good enough and when we can move on, so in other words GEMO. Good enough, move on!

Why Practice Out Loud?

Memory reinforcement happens when you speak your answers aloud, this can also happen when you write down your answers with a pen and piece of paper. Typing your answers is not as effective for memory. Also, it helps you internalize the content and recall it more easily during the interview.

Fluency and Clarity:

Verbal practice ensures that your responses flow smoothly, sounds good, and lets you refine the message. Also, it prevents stumbling or hesitating during the actual interview.

Confidence Boost:

Hearing yourself articulate ideas boosts confidence, clarity, and tone. You will feel more prepared and assured, which in turn builds confidence.

Record Yourself:

Use your phone or a voice recorder. Answer common interview questions as if you're in an actual interview. Listen to the recording and assess your clarity, tone, and pacing.

Role-Play with a Friend:

Enlist a friend or family member to play the interviewer.

Practice answering questions together. Their feedback can

be invaluable.

Mirror Practice:

Stand in front of a mirror and deliver your answers.

Observe your body language, facial expressions, and

gestures.

Time Yourself:

Interviews have time constraints. Practice within the

allotted time. Concise answers leave a stronger impact.

Tips for Effective Practice:

Eye Contact:

Even when practicing alone, maintain eye contact with an imaginary interviewer. It builds confidence and helps you to connect with the interviewer. If you have a hard time look right into their eyes, then focus on the space between the eyes.

Vary Your Tone:

Avoid monotone delivery in everything you do, especially in an interview. If you are a bore, the poor interviewer may end the interview early. Try to emphasize key points and modulate your voice, also consider adding a "pause" occasionally. Nothing will grab your audience's attention like a pause, for suspense.

Stay Positive:

Frame your answers positively and focus on solutions, growth, and success. Nothing kills an interview than a "Debbie Downer" answers all the questions with negative outcomes. Ish, I would not want that type of person working for me, would you? Don't do it!

Feedback Loop:

Continuously improve based on feedback. Adjust your responses as needed. Remember, practicing out loud transforms theoretical knowledge into practical skills. The more you rehearse, the better prepared you'll be to ace those interviews!

Chapter 7: Thoughtful Questions

Asking thoughtful questions at the end of an interview not only demonstrates your interest but also helps you gather essential information. This also can show your intelligence and how you prepared for the interview. When I interview a candidate, I like to know that they researched the company, and have some good questions.

Here's how to approach it:

Role-Related Questions:

Q "What are the day-to-day responsibilities of this role?": Understand the specific tasks you'll be handling.

Q "What are the short-term and long-term goals for this position?": This shows your commitment to contributing effectively.

Q "How does success in this role impact the overall team or company?": Highlight your desire to make a meaningful difference.

Team Dynamics Questions:

Q "Can you describe the team structure?": Learn about reporting lines, collaboration, and team size.

Q "What's the team's communication style?": Understand if they prefer regular meetings, Slack, or other channels.

"How does the team handle conflict or disagreements?": Gauge their approach to teamwork.

Company Culture Questions:

Q "What values does the company prioritize?": Align your personal values with theirs.

Q "How does the company support employee growth and development?": Show your interest in continuous learning.

Q "What social activities or events does the company organize?": Learn about team bonding opportunities.

Industry and Market Questions (Optional):

Q "What challenges or trends is the industry currently facing?": Display awareness and curiosity.

Q "How does the company stay competitive in this market?": Understand their strategies.

Remember, thoughtful questions not only provide valuable insights but also leave a positive impression on the interviewer. Be genuine, engaged, and curious!

Chapter 8: Psychological Tips to Win

Here are some psychological tips to help you succeed in a job interview:

Schedule Your Interview Strategically:

Aim for around 10:30 a.m. on a Tuesday. This is when interviewers are likely to be more relaxed and attentive. Avoid early mornings (when they're busy) or late afternoons (when they're mentally winding down).

Be Mindful of Color Psychology:

- Blue: Conveys teamwork, loyalty, trust, and reliability.
- Black: Suggests leadership potential.
- Orange: Avoid—it's seen as unprofessional

Remote Interviews:

For remote interviews, make sure to maintain eye level with the camera, if you are looking up at the camera, I have found that this can be interpreted as worship and looking down is shame. So, keep the camera at eye level.

Tailor Your Answers to the Interviewer's Age:

Adapt your language and examples based on whether your interview is older or younger. This can help to make the interviewer understand your point of view. We tend to like hearing information in our own language, or the way we communicate. Try to connect on shared experiences or generational perspectives.

Visual Queues

Recommended to all my clients, because I feel that this is a key tip, let your interviewer see that you are taking notes. Either tell them you are taking notes or let them see you writing on a pad. Now, this is key. It has to be a pen and paper, not typing on a laptop. This signals to the interviewer that you care about what they have to say, you are interested, and you want to learn.

Use Open Body Language:

Open bod language sends signals of trust, honesty, and makes you more approachable.

Palms open: Indicates honesty and openness.

Steeple your hands: Shows confidence and authority.

Find Common Ground:

Discover shared interests or experiences with your interviewer. Personally, I like to do a little cyber research and see if I can find some common ground before the interview. I also look to see if we know anyone in common, a quick message from a friend to the interviewer can help to pave the way for a more enjoyable interview.

Visualize Success:

Try to visualize yourself completing a successful interview, in a role you want, and full of confidence. This activity can help to release dopamine, which can boost your confidence.

Remember, interviews are not just about skills; they're about connecting with people. Use these psychological tricks to leave a lasting impression!

Chapter 9: Get that right salary!

Most of the time, when you interview for a position, you will be asked for your expected salary range. If you give them a range that is too high, they may think that you are too expensive for them. If you give them a range too low, they may think that you do not have the experience. I strongly recommend that you do proper research first, go to salary.com or another website like Glassdoor. These sites have information on the current positions at the company and their annual salary. Plus, these websites can also provide benefits information.

Be ready to discuss salary expectations when the interviewer asks you about your desired compensation. Use tools like Indeed's Salary Calculator to determine an appropriate range based on your location and experience. This will help you avoid asking for too much or too little and show that you have done your research. You can also mention other factors that influence your salary expectations, such as benefits, bonuses, or relocation assistance. Be prepared to negotiate if the offer does not meet your expectations, but also be respectful and realistic.

Negotiating salary can be nerve-wracking, but with the right approach, you can advocate for fair compensation. Here are key strategies to help you negotiate your salary effectively:

Start by Evaluating What You Have to Offer:

Understand your value to the employer and consider all factors like:

- Geographic location: Cost of living varies; adjust your expectations accordingly. Cost of gas to get to the job

- Industry experience: More experience may warrant a higher salary. How about a certification? Advanced degree? All of these can boost your worth!

- Leadership experience: If you meet or exceed leadership expectations, it justifies higher pay.

- Education level: Relevant degrees impact compensation.

- Career level: Advancing in your career often correlates with higher pay

- Technical experience: Have you used any software systems that could be valuable experience?

Research the Market Average:

Use tools like Indeed's Salary Calculator to determine industry standards for your role and location.

Armed with this data, you'll know what's reasonable to ask for.

Prepare Your Talking Points:

Create a list of reasons why you deserve the salary you're requesting. Highlight your skills, achievements, and unique contributions.

Schedule a Time to Discuss:

Arrange a meeting to discuss salary face-to-face.

Avoid busy Mondays or lunch hours for a focused

conversation

Rehearse with a Trusted Friend:

Practice your negotiation points out loud and by

rehearsing, you will boost confidence and help you

articulate your case effectively.

Be Confident:

Approach the negotiation with a positive mindset.

Confidence leaves a lasting impression on the hiring

manager.

Lead with Gratitude:

Express appreciation for the job offers, thank your future

employer for their time and attention during your

interview process, and then transition into the salary

discussion.

Ask for the Top of Your Range:

Present a salary range rather than a fixed number.

Start with the higher end of your range to allow room for negotiation.

Remember, salary negotiation is a two-way conversation. Be respectful, assertive, and willing to compromise. If the employer can't meet your minimum requirements, don't hesitate to walk away. Your worth matters!

Conclusion

Personally, having given and reviewed thousands of interviews and resumes, over the last 25 years, I have found by giving an interview has helped me with my understanding of the entire process. Doctors should always practice being a patient, same with lawyers, accountants, it can help open your perspective.

So, this is another idea, in conclusion, interview your friends for the job you want, and you may notice some distinct aspects. Are you paying attention to the body language of the person you are interviewing? How do you feel when you see their face? Now that you have a better understanding of how to interview, it is imperative that you practice, and push yourself to improve. This is a skill, just like any other, don't expect yourself to rock your first interview, but you will by the 5th!

Good luck and happy interviewing!

Freebies

JobScan.co – get 10 free scans of your resume and job description for match.

https://www.jobscan.co?ref=2783844&utm_source=referral-program&utm_medium=referral&utm_campaign=10-scan-referral-program

Get 20% off your coaching session with CoreTactic. We can help prepare you for your interview, practice with you, record your interviews for review, and help you refine your elevator pitch.

APPENDIX A: References

LinkedIn, https://www.linkedin.com

Glassdoor, https://www.glassdoor.com

LinkedIn Sales Navigator,

https://www.linkedin.com/sales

Everything You Need to Know About Answering Behavioral Interview Questions, https://www.themuse.com/advice/behavioral-interview-questions-answers-examples, Accessed 2/12/2024

21+ Behavioral Interview Questions in 2024 (+Sample Answers) https://novoresume.com/career-blog/behavioral-interview-questions, Accessed 2/12/2024

50 TOP BEHAVIORAL INTERVIEW QUESTIONS TO ASK CANDIDATES https://www.apollotechnical.com/behavioral-interview-questions/, Accessed 1/24/2024

25 Psychology Interview Questions (With Answer Examples)

https://www.indeed.com/career-advice/interviewing/interview-questions-psychology, Accessed 2/2/2024

How to Answer the 3 Trickiest Job Interview Questions, Remember: You're evaluating them, too., https://www.psychologytoday.com/us/blog/tame-your-terrible-office-tyrant/202311/the-3-trickiest-job-interview-questions-and-best, Accessed 2/10/2024

Interview and Job Talk Tips, https://www.apa.org/education-career/job-search/interview-negotiate/tips, Accessed 2/11/2024

SURPRISE BONUS CHAPTER

The largest list of Behavioral Interview Questions ever assembled!

Adaptability

- Describe a major change that occurred in a job that you held. How did you adapt to this change? Tell us about a situation in which you had to adjust to changes over which you had no control.
- How did you handle it?
- Tell us about a time that you had to adapt to a difficult situation.
- What do you do when priorities change quickly? Give one example of when this happened.

Ambition

- Describe a project or idea that was implemented primarily because of your efforts. What was your role? What was the outcome?
- Describe a time when you suggested to improve the work in your organization. Give an example of an important goal that you set in the past. Tell about your success in reaching it.

- Give two examples of things you've done in previous jobs that demonstrate your willingness to work hard.

- How many hours a day do you put into your work? What were your study patterns at school? Tell us about a time when you had to go above and beyond the call of duty to get a job done.

- Tell us about a time when a job had to be completed and you were able to focus your attention and efforts to get it done.

- Tell us about a time when you were particularly effective on prioritizing tasks and completing a project on schedule.

- Tell us about the last time that you undertook a project that demanded a lot of initiative.

- Tell us how you keep your job knowledge current with the on-going changes in the industry.

- There are times when we work without close supervision or support to get the job done. Tell us about a time when you found yourself in such a situation and how things turned out.

- What impact did you have in your last job?

- What is the most competitive work situation you have experienced? How did you handle it? What was the result?

- What is the riskiest decision you have made? What was the situation? What happened? What kinds of challenges did you face on your last job? Give an example of how you handled them.

- What projects have you started on your own recently? What prompted you to get started?

- What sorts of things have you done to become better qualified for your career?

- What was the best idea that you came up with in your career? How did you apply it?

- When you disagree with your manager, what do you do? Give an example.

- When you have a lot of work to do, how do you get it all done? Give an example.

Analytical Thinking

- Describe the project or situation which best demonstrates your analytical abilities. What was your role?

- Developing and using a detailed procedure is often very important in a job. Tell about a time when you needed to develop and use a detailed procedure to successfully complete a project.

- Give a specific example of a time when you used good judgment and login in solving a problem. Give me a specific example of a time when you used good judgment and logic in solving a problem.

- Give me an example of when you took a risk to achieve a goal. What was the outcome?

- How did you go about making the changes (step by step)? Answer in depth or detail such as "What were you thinking at that point?" or "Tell me more about meeting with that person", or "Lead me through your decision process".

- Relate a specific instance when you found it necessary to be precise in your work.

- Tell us about a job or setting where great precision to detail was required to complete a task.

- How did you handle that situation?

- Tell us about a time when you had to analyse information and make a recommendation. What kind of thought process did you go through? What was your reasoning behind your decision?

- Tell us about your experience in past jobs that required you to be especially alert to details while doing the task involved.

Building Relationships

- Give a specific example of a time when you had to address an angry customer. What was the problem and what was the outcome? How would you asses your role in diffusing the situation?

- It is very important to build good relationships at work but sometimes it doesn't always work. If you can, talk about a time when you were not able to build a successful relationship with a difficult person.

- Tell us about a time when you built rapport quickly with someone under difficult conditions. What, in your opinion, are the key ingredients in guiding and maintaining successful business relationships? Give examples of how you made these work for you.

Business Systems Thinking

- Describe how your position contributes to your organization's/unit's goals. What are the unit's goals/mission?
- Tell us about a politically complex work situation in which you worked.

Caution

- Have you ever worked in a situation where the rules and guidelines were not clear? Tell me about it. How did you feel about it? How did you react?
- Some people consider themselves to be "big picture people" and others are "detail oriented".

- Which are you? Give an example of a time when you displayed this.
- Tell us me about a situation when it was important for you to pay attention to details. How did you handle it?
- Tell us me about a time when you demonstrated too much initiative?

Communication

- Describe a situation in which you were able to effectively "read" another person and guide your actions by your understanding of their individual needs or values.
- Describe a situation when you were able to strengthen a relationship by communicating effectively. What made your communication effective?
- Describe a situation where you felt you had not communicated well. How did you correct the situation?

- Describe a time when you were able to effectively communicate a difficult or unpleasant idea to a superior.

- Describe the most significant written document, report, or presentation which you had to complete.

- Give me an example of a time when you were able to successfully communicate with another person, even when that individual may not have personally liked you, or vice versa.

- Give me an example of a time when you were able to successfully communicate with another person, even when that individual may not have personally liked you.

- Have you ever had to "sell" an idea to your co-workers or group? How did you do it? Did they "buy" it?

- Have you had to "sell" an idea to your co-workers, classmates, or group? How did you do it? Did they "buy" it?

- How do you keep subordinates informed about information that affects their jobs?

- How do you keep your manager informed about what is being done in your work area? How do you go about explaining a complex technical problem to a person who does not understand technical jargon? What approach do you take in communicating with people?

- What kinds of communication situations cause you difficulty? Give an example.

- Tell us about a recent successful experience in making a speech or presentation. How did you prepare? What obstacles did you face? How did you handle them?

- Tell us about a time when you and your current/previous supervisor disagreed but you still found a way to get your point across.

- Tell us about a time when you had to present complex information. How did you ensure that the other person understood?

- Tell us about a time when you had to use your verbal communication skills to get a point across that was important to you.

- Tell us about a time when you were particularly effective in a talk you gave or a seminar you taught.
- Tell us about an experience in which you had to speak up to be sure that other people knew what you thought or felt.
- Tell us me about a situation when you had to speak up (be assertive) to get a point across that was important to you.
- Tell us me about a time in which you had to use your written communication skills to get an important point across.
- What challenges have occurred while you were coordinating work with other units, departments, and/or divisions?
- What have you done to improve your verbal communication skills?
- How have you persuaded people through a document you prepared?
- What are the most challenging documents you have done? What kinds of proposals have your written?

- What kinds of writing have you done? How do you prepare written communications?

Conflict Resolution

- Describe a time when you took personal accountability for a conflict and initiated contact with the individual(s) involved to explain your actions.

Customer Orientation

- How do you handle problems with customers? Give an example.

- How do you go about establishing rapport with a customer? What have you done to gain their confidence? Give an example.

- What have you done to improve relations with your customers?

Decision Making

- Discuss an important decision you have made regarding a task or project at work. What factors influenced your decision?

- Everyone has made some poor decisions or has done something that just did not turn out right.

- Has this happened to you? What happened?
- Give an example of a time in which you had to be relatively quick in coming to a decision. Give an example of a time in which you had to keep from speaking or not finish a task because you did not have enough information to come to a good decision. Give an example of a time when there was a decision to be made and procedures were not in place?
- Give an example of a time when you had to be relatively quick in coming to a decision. Give me an example of a time when you had to keep from speaking or deciding because you did not have enough information.
- How did you go about deciding what strategy to employ when dealing with a difficult customer?
- How do you go about developing I information to decide? Give an example.
- How do you involve your manager and/or others when you decide?

- How have you gone about making important decisions?
- How quickly do you make decisions? Give an example.
- In a current job task, what steps do you go through to ensure your decisions are correct/effective?
- Tell us about a time when you had to defend a decision you made even though other important people were opposed to your decision.
- What kind of decisions do you make rapidly? What kind takes more time? Give examples. What kinds of problems have you had coordinating technical projects? How did you solve t hem?
- What was your most difficult decision in the last 6 months? What made it difficult? When you must make a highly technical decision, how do you go about doing it?

Delegation

- Do you consider yourself a macro or micro manager? How do you delegate?
- How do you make the decision to delegate work?

- Tell us how you go about delegating work?
- What was the biggest mistake you have had when delegating work? The biggest success?

Detail-Oriented

- Describe a situation where you had the option to leave the details to others or you could take care of them yourself.
- Do prefer to work with the "big picture" or the "details" of a situation? Give me an example of an experience that illustrates your preference.
- Have the jobs you held in the past required little attention, moderate attention, or a great deal of attention to detail? Give me an example of a situation that illustrates this requirement. Tell us about a difficult experience you had in working with details.
- Tell us about a situation where attention to detail was either important or unimportant in accomplishing an assigned task.

Employee Development

- Tell us about a training program that you have developed or enhanced.
- Evaluating Alternatives
- Have you ever had a situation where you had several alternatives to choose from? How did you go about choosing one?
- How did you assemble the information?
- How did you review the information? What process did you follow to reach a conclusion?
- What alternatives did you develop?
- What are some of the major decisions you have made over the past (6, 12, 18) months? What kinds of decisions are most difficult for you? Describe one? Who made the decision?

Flexibility

- Have you ever had a subordinate whose performance was consistently marginal? What did you do?
- How have you adjusted your style when it was not meeting the objectives and/or people were not responding correctly?

- What do you do when you are faced with an obstacle to an important project? Give an example. When you have difficulty persuading someone to your point of view, what do you do? Give an example.

Follow-up and Control

- How did you keep track of delegated assignments?
- How do you evaluate the productivity/effectiveness of your subordinates?
- How do you get data for performance reviews?
- How do you keep track of what your subordinates are doing?
- What administrative paperwork do you have? Is it useful? Why/why not?

Initiative

- Give me an example of when you had to go above and beyond the call of duty to get a job done.
- Give me examples of projects/tasks you started on your own.

- Give some instances in which you anticipated problems and were able to influence a new direction.

- How did you get work assignments at your most recent employer?

- What changes did you develop at your most recent employer?

- What kinds of things really get your excited?

- What sorts of projects did you generate that required you to go beyond your job description? What sorts of things did you do at school that were beyond expectations?

Interpersonal Skills

- Describe a recent unpopular decision you made and what the result was.

- Describe a recent unpopular decision you made and what the result was.

- Describe a situation in which you were able to effectively "read" another person and guide your actions by your understanding of their needs and values.

- Tell us about the most difficult or frustrating individual that you've ever had to work with, and how you managed to work with them.
- What have you done in past situations to contribute toward a teamwork environment? What have you done in the past to contribute toward a teamwork environment?

Innovation

- Can you think of a situation where innovation was required at work? What did you do in this situation?
- Describe a situation when you demonstrated initiative and acted without waiting for direction. What was the outcome?
- Describe a time when you came up with a creative solution/idea/project/report to a problem in your past work.
- Describe something that you have implemented at work. What were the steps used to implement this?
- Describe the most creative work-related project which you have carried out.

- Give me an example of when you took a risk to achieve a goal. What was the outcome?

- Sometimes it is essential that we break out of the routine, standardized way of doing things to complete the task. Give an example of when you were able to successfully develop such a new approach.

- Tell us about a problem that you solved in a unique or unusual way. What was the outcome? Were you satisfied with it?

- Tell us about a suggestion you made to improve the way job processes/operations worked. What was the result?

- There are many jobs in which well-established methods are typically followed. Give a specific example of a time when you tried some other method to do the job.

- There are many jobs that require creative or innovative thinking. Give an example of when you had such a job and how you handled it.

- What have been some of your most creative ideas?

- What innovative procedures have you developed? How did you develop them? Who was involved? Where did the ideas come from?

- What new or unusual ideas have you developed on your job? How did you develop them? What was the result? Did you implement them?

- When was the last time that you thought "outside of the box" and how did you do it?

Integrity

- Describe a time when you were asked to keep information confidential.

- Give examples of how you have acted with integrity in your job/work relationship. If you can, tell us about a time when your trustworthiness was challenged. How did you react/respond?

- On occasion we are confronted by dishonesty in the workplace. Tell about such an occurrence and how you handled it.

- Tell us about a specific time when you had to handle a tough problem which challenged fairness or ethnical issues.

- Trust requires personal accountability. Can you tell us about a time when you chose to trust someone? What was the outcome?

Introducing Change

- Have you ever had to introduce a policy change to your work group? How did you do it? Have you ever met resistance when implementing a new idea or policy to a work group? How did you deal with it? What happened?
- When is the last time you had to introduce a new idea or procedure to people on this job? How did you do it?

Leadership

- Give an example of a time in which you felt you were able to build motivation in your co-workers or subordinates at work.
- Give an example of your ability to build motivation in your co-workers, classmates, and even if on a volunteer committee.

- Have you ever had difficulty getting others to accept your ideas? What was your approach? Did it work?
- Have you ever been a member of a group where two of the members did not work well together? What did you do to get them to do so?
- What is the toughest group that you have had to get cooperation from?
- What is the toughest group that you have had to get cooperation from? Describe how you handled it. What was the outcome?

Listening

- Give an example of a time when you made a mistake because you did not listen well to what someone had to say.
- How often do you have to rely on information you have gathered from others when talking to them? What kinds of problems have you had? What happened?
- What do you do to show people that you are listing to them?

- When is listening important on your job? When is listening difficult?

Motivating Others

- Have you ever had a subordinate whose work was always marginal? How did you deal with that person? What happened?
- How do you deal with people whose work exceeds your expectations?
- How do you get subordinates to produce at a high level? Give an example.
- How do you get subordinates to work at their peak potential? Give an example. How do you manage cross-functional teams?

Motivation

- Describe a situation when you were able to have a positive influence on the actions of others.
- Give an example of a time when you went above and beyond the call of duty.
- Give me an example of a time when you went above and beyond the call of duty.

- How would you define "success" for someone in your chosen career?
- Tell us me about an important goal that you set in the past. Were you successful? Why?

Negotiating

- Describe the most challenging negotiation in which you were involved. What did you do? What were the results for you? What were the results for the other party?
- Have you ever been in a situation where you had to bargain with someone? How did you feel about this? What did you do? Give an example.
- How did you prepare for it?
  How did you present your position?
- How did you resolve it?
- Tell us about the last time you had to negotiate with someone. What was the most difficult part?

Organizational

- Describe a time when you had to make a difficult choice between your personal and professional life.

- Give me an example of a project that best describes your organizational skills.
- How do you decide what gets top priority when scheduling your time?
- What do you do when your schedule is suddenly interrupted? Give an example.

Performance Management
- Give an example of a time when you helped a staff member accept change and make the necessary adjustments to move forward. What were the change/transition skills that you used.
- Give an example of how you have been successful at empowering either a person or a group of people into accomplishing a task.
- How do you handle a subordinate whose work is not up to expectations?
- How do you coach a subordinate to develop a new skill?

- How do you handle performance reviews? Tell me about a difficult one.

- How often do you discuss a subordinate's performance with him/her? Give an example. Tell us about a specific development plan that you created and carried out with one or more of your employees. What was the specific situation? What were the components of the development plan? What was the outcome?

- Tell us about a time when you had to take disciplinary action with someone you supervised. Tell us about a time when you had to tell a staff member that you were dissatisfied with his or her work.

- Tell us about a time when you had to use your authority to get something done. Where there any negative consequences?

- There are times when people need extra help. Give an example of when you were able to provide that support to a person with whom you worked.

- What have you done to develop the skills of your staff?
- When do you give positive feedback to people? Tell me about the last time you did. Give an example of how you handle the need for constructive criticism with a subordinate or peer.

Personal Effectiveness

- Give an example of a situation where others were intense, but you were able to maintain your composure.
- It is important to maintain a positive attitude at work when you have other things on your mind.
- Give a specific example of when you were able to do that.
- Keeping others informed of your progress/actions helps them feel comfortable. Tell your methods for keeping your supervisor advised of the status on projects.
- Tell us about a recent job or experience that you would describe as a real learning experience?
- What did you learn from the job or experience?

- Tell us about a time when you took responsibility for an error and were held personally accountable.
- Tell us about a time when your supervisor criticized your work. How did you respond?
- Tell us about some demanding situations in which you managed to remain calm and composed. There are times when we are placed under extreme pressure on the job. Tell about a time when you were under such pressure and how you handled it.
- What have you done to further your own professional development in the past 5 years.
- When you have been made aware of, or have discovered for yourself, a problem in your work performance, what was your course of action? Can you give an example?

Persuasion

- Describe a situation in which you were able to positively influence the actions of others in a desired direction.

- Describe a situation where you were able to use persuasion to successfully convince someone to see things your way.

- Describe a time when you were able to convince a sceptical or resistant customer to purchase a project or utilize your services.

- Have you ever had to persuade a group to accept a proposal or idea? How did you go about doing it? What was the result?

- Have you ever had to persuade a peer or manager to accept an idea that you knew they would not like? Describe the resistance you met and how you overcame it.

- How do you get a peer or colleague to accept one of your ideas?

- In selling an idea, it is sometimes useful to use metaphors, analogies, or stories to make your point. Give a recent example of when you were able to successfully do that.

- Tell us about a time when you had to convince someone in authority about your ideas. How did it work out?

- Tell us about a time when you used facts and reason to persuade someone to accept your recommendation.

- Tell us about a time when you used your leadership ability to gain support for what initially had strong opposition.

- Tell us about a time when you were able to successfully influence another person.

Planning and Organization

- Describe how you develop a project team's goals and project plan?

- How do you schedule your time? Set priorities? How do you handle doing twenty things at once?

- What do you do when your time schedule or project plan is upset by unforeseen circumstances?

- Give an example.

- What have you done to be effective with your organization and planning?

Presentation

- How do you prepare for a presentation to a group of technical experts in your field?

- How would you describe your presentation style?

- Tell us about the most effective presentation you have made. What was the topic? What made it difficult? How did you handle it?

- What kinds of oral presentations have you made? How did you prepare for them? What challenges did you have?

Problem Solving

- Describe the most difficult working relationship you've had with an individual. What specific actions did you take to improve the relationship? What was the outcome?

- Give me an example of a situation where you had difficulties with a team member. What, if anything, did you do to resolve the difficulties?

- Have you ever been caught unaware by a problem or obstacles that you had not foreseen? What happened?

- Tell us about a time when you did something completely different from the plan and/or assignment. Why? What happened?
- What are some of the problems you have faced, such as between business development and project leaders, between one department and another, between you and your peers? How did you recognize that they were there?
- When was the last time something came up in a meeting that was not covered in the plan? What did you do? What were the results of your judgment?

Problem Resolution

- Describe a situation where you had a conflict with another individual, and how you dealt with it.
- What was the outcome? How do you feel about it?
- Describe a time in which you were faced with problems or stresses which tested your coping skills. What did you do?
- Describe a time when you facilitated a creative solution to a problem between two employees.

- Give a specific example of a time when you used good judgment and logic in solving a problem. Give an example of a problem which you faced on any job that you have had and tell how you went about solving it.

- Give an example of when you "went to the source" to address a conflict. Do you feel trust levels were improved as a result?

- Problems occur in almost all work relationships. Describe a time when you had to cope with the resentment or hostility of a subordinate or co-worker.

- Some problems require developing a unique approach. Tell about a time when you were able to develop a different problem-solving approach.

- Sometimes the only way to resolve a defense or conflict is through negotiation and compromise. Tell about a time when you were able to resolve a difficult situation by finding some common ground.

- Sometimes we need to remain calm on the outside when we are really upset on the inside. Give an example of a time that this happened to you.
- Tell us about a recent success you had with an especially difficult employee/co-worker. Tell us about a situation in which you had to separate the person from the issue when working to resolve issues.
- Tell us about a time when you identified a potential problem and resolved the situation before it became serious.
- There is more than one way to solve a problem. Give an example from your recent work experience that would illustrate this.

Project Management

- Tell us about a time when you influenced the outcome of a project by taking a leadership role.
- Using a specific example of a project, tell how you kept those involved informed of the progress.

Relate Well

- Describe a situation where you had to use conflict management skills.

- Describe a situation where you had to use confrontation skills.

- Give me an example of a time when a company policy or action hurt people. What, if anything, did you do to mitigate the negative consequences to people?

- How do you typically deal with conflict? Can you give me an example?

- Tell us about a time when you were forced to make an unpopular decision.

- What would your co-workers (or staff) stay be the most frustrating thing about your communications with them?

Removing Obstacles

- Have you ever dealt with a situation where communications were poor? Where there was a lack of cooperation? Lack of trust? How did you handle these situations?

- What do you do when a subordinate comes to you with a challenge?
- What have you done to help your subordinates to be more productive?
- What have you done to make sure that your subordinates can be productive? Give an example.

Resolving Conflict

- Have you ever been in a situation where you had to settle an argument between two friends (or people you knew)? What did you do? What was the result?
- Have you ever had to settle conflict between two people on the job? What was the situation and what did you do?
- Tell us about a time when you had to help two peers settle a dispute. How did you go about identifying the issues? What did you do? What was the result?
- Resource Management
- Tell us about a time when you organized or planned an event that was very successful.

Scheduling

- Describe the most difficult scheduling problem you have faced.
- How did you assign priorities to jobs?
- How did you go about making job assignments?
- When all have been over-loaded, how do your people meet job assignments?

Self-Assessment

- Can you recall a time when you were less than pleased with your performance?
- Describe a situation in which you were able to use persuasion to successfully convince someone to see things your way.
- Give me a specific occasion in which you conformed to a policy with which you did not agree. Give me an example of an important goal that your h ad set in the past and tell me about your success in reaching it.
- If there were one area you've always wanted to improve upon, what would that be?
- In what ways are you trying to improve yourself?

- Tell us about a time when you had to go above and beyond the call of duty to get a job done.
- What do you consider to be your professional strengths? Give me a specific example using this attribute in the workplace.
- What goal have you set for yourself that you have successfully achieved? What was the most useful criticism you ever received?

Selecting and Developing People

- How do you coach an employee in completing a new assignment?
- What have you done to develop your subordinates? Give an example.
- What have you done to improve the skills of your subordinates?
- What was your biggest mistake in hiring someone? What happened? How did you deal with the situation?
- What was your biggest success in hiring someone? What did you do?

Setting Goals

- Did you have a strategic plan? How was it developed? How did you communicate it to the rest of your staff?

- How do you communicate goals to subordinates? Give an example.

- How do you involve people in developing your unit's goals? Give an example.

- What company plans have you developed? Which ones have you reached? How did you reach them? Which have you missed? Why did you miss them?

- What goals did you miss? Why did you miss them?

- What goals have you met? What did you do to meet them?

- What were your annual goals at your most current employer? How did you develop these goals? What were your long-range plans at your most recent employer? What was our role in developing them?

- Setting Performance Standards

- How do you go about setting goals with subordinates? How do you involve them in this process?

- How do you let subordinates know what you expect of them?

- What performance standards do you have for your unit? How have you communicated them to your subordinates?

Setting Priorities

- Have you ever been overloaded with work? How do you keep track of work so that it gets done on time?

- How do you manage your time?

- How do you schedule your time?

- When given an important assignment, how do you approach it?

Sound Judgment

- Describe a situation when you had to exercise a significant amount of self-control.

- Give me an example of a time in which you had to be relatively quick in coming to a decision. Give me an example of when you were able to meet the personal and professional demands in your life yet still maintained a healthy balance.

- Give me an example of when you were responsible for an error or mistake. What was the outcome? What, if anything, would you do differently?

- If you were interviewing for this position, what would you be looking for in the applicants? We work with a great deal of confidential information. Describe how you would have handled sensitive information in a past work experience. What strategies would you utilize to maintain confidentiality when pressured by others?

- When have you had to produce results without sufficient guidelines? Give an example.

Strategic Planning

- Describe what steps/methods you have used to define/identify a vision for your unit/position.

- How do you see your job relating to the overall goals of the organization?

- In your current or former position, what were your long and short-term goals? Tell us about a time when you anticipated the future and made changes to current responsibilities/operations to meet future needs.

Stress Management

- How did you react when faced with constant time pressure? Give an example.
- People react differently when job demands are constantly changing; how do you react?
- What kind of events cause you stress on the job?
- What was the most stressful situation you have faced? How did you deal with it?

Teamwork

- Describe a situation in which you had to arrive at a compromise or help others to compromise.
- What was your role? What steps did you take? What was the result?
- Describe a team experience you found disappointing. What would you have done to prevent this?
- Describe a team experience you found rewarding.

- Describe the types of teams you've been involved with. What were your roles?
- Describe your leadership style and give an example of a situation when you successfully led a group.
- Give an example of how you have been successful at empowering a group of people in accomplishing a task.
- Give an example of how you worked effectively with people to accomplish an important result. Have you ever been a project leader? Give examples of problems you experienced and how you reacted.
- Have you ever been in a position where you had to lead a group of peers? How did you handle it?
- Have you ever participated in a task group? What was your role? How did you contribute? Please give your best example of working cooperatively as a team member to accomplish an important goal. What was the goal or objective? To what extent did you interact with others on this project?

- Some people work best as part of a group - others prefer the role of individual contributor. How would you describe yourself? Give an example of a situation where you felt you were most effective.
- Tell us about a time that you had to work on a team that did not get along. What happened?
- What role did you take? What was the result?
- Tell us about a work experience where you had to work closely with others. How did it go? How did you overcome any difficulties?
- Tell us about the most difficult challenge you faced in trying to work cooperatively with someone who did not share the same ideas? What was your role in achieving the work objective?
- Tell us about the most difficult situation you have had when leading a team. What happened and what did you do? Was it successful? Emphasize the "single" most important thing you did?
- Tell us about the most effective contribution you have made as part of a task group or special project team.

- Think about the times you have been a team leader. What could you have done to be more effective?

- What is the difficult part of being a member, not leader, of a team? How did you handle this? What role have you typically played as a member of a team? How did you interact with other members of the team?

- When is the last time you had a disagreement with a peer? How did you resolve the situation?

- When working on a team project have you ever had an experience where there was strong disagreement among team members? What did you do?

Time Management Schedule

- Describe a situation that required you to do several things at the same time. How did you handle it? What was the result?

- How do you determine priorities in scheduling your time? Give an example.

- How do you typically plan your day to manage your time effectively?

- Of your current assignments, which do you consider having required the greatest amount of effort about planning/organization? How have you accomplished this assignment? How would you asses your effectiveness?

Toughness

- On many occasions, managers must make tough decisions. What was the most difficult one you have had to make?

- Tell us about setbacks you have faced. How did you deal with them?

- What has been your major work-related disappointment? What happened and what did you do? What is the most competitive situation you have experienced? How did you handle it? What was the result? What was your major disappointment?

Variety

- How many projects do you work on at once? Please describe.

- When was the last time you made a key decision on the spur of the moment? What was the reason and result?

- When was the last time you were in a crisis? What was the situation? How did you react? Which of your jobs had the most rapid change? How did you feel about it?

Values Diversity

- Give a specific example of how you have helped create an environment where differences are valued, encouraged, and supported.

- Tell us about a time that you successfully adapted to a culturally different environment. Tell us about a time when you had to adapt to a wide variety of people by accepting/understanding their perspective.

- Tell us about a time when you made an intentional effort to get to know someone from another culture.

- What have you done to further your knowledge/understanding about diversity? How have you demonstrated your learning?

- What have you done to support diversity in your unit?
- What measures have you taken to make someone feel comfortable in an environment that was obviously uncomfortable?

www.ingramcontent.com/pod-product-compliance
Lightning Source LLC
Chambersburg PA
CBHW071052290526
45795CB00004B/1447